# PARASITES

# PARASITES

HOWARD AND MARGERY FACKLAM

**TWENTY-FIRST CENTURY BOOKS**

A DIVISION OF HENRY HOLT AND COMPANY

NEW YORK

Twenty-First Century Books
A Division of Henry Holt and Company, Inc.
115 West 18th Street
New York, NY 10011

Henry Holt ® and colophon are trademarks of
Henry Holt and Company, Inc.
*Publishers since 1866*

Text Copyright © 1994 Howard and Margery Facklam
All rights reserved.
Published in Canada by Fitzhenry & Whiteside Ltd.
195 Allstate Parkway, Markham, Ontario L3R 4T8

**Library of Congress Cataloging-in-Publication Data**
Facklam, Howard.
      Parasites / Howard and Margery Facklam. — 1st ed.
          p. cm. — (Invaders)
      Includes bibliographical references (p.   ) and index.
      1. Host–parasite relationships—Juvenile literature. 2. Parasites—
Juvenile literature. [1. Parasites] I. Facklam, Margery. II. Title. III.
Series.
      QL757.F23  1994
      574.5'249—dc20                                                          94-25431
                                                                                                        CIP
                                                                                                        AC
ISBN 0-8050-2858-7
First Edition 1994

Printed in the United States of America
All first editions are printed on acid-free paper ∞.

10  9  8  7  6  5  4  3  2  1

### Photo Credits

Cover: Brice Coleman Agency; p. 8: Gregory Demijian/Photo Researchers,
Inc.; p. 8 (inset): M. Abbey Photo/Science Source/Photo Researchers,
Inc.; p. 11: C. Ah Rider/Photo Researchers, Inc.; p. 13: Gilbert Grant/Photo
Researchers, Inc.; p. 15: Allen Tannenbaum/Sygma; p. 17: The Bettmann
Archive; p. 20: Tom McHugh/Photo Researchers, Inc.; p. 22: J. L.
Charmet/SPL/Science Source/Photo Researchers, Inc.; p. 24: J. H.
Robinson/Photo Researchers Inc.; p. 26: Dr. J. Burgess/SPL/Science
Source/Photo Researchers, Inc.; p. 30: Sinclair Stammers/SPL/Science
Source/Photo Researchers, Inc.; p. 33: Dallas and John Heaton/Westlight;
p. 35: R. Calentine/Visuals Unlimited; pp. 38, 40: Ed Reschke/Peter
Arnold; p. 43: Chris Bjornborg/Science Source/Photo Researchers, Inc.; p.
45: Astrid and Hans Frieder– Michler/SPL/Science Source/Photo
Researchers, Inc.; p. 47: CNRI/SPL/Science Source/Photo Researchers,
Inc.; p. 49: Culver Pictures; p. 52: Raymond A. Mendez/Animals Animals;
p. 54: Peter Arnold, Inc.; p. 56: Breck P. Kent.

# CONTENTS

# 1

# EATING FOR TWO

Imagine having parasites in your eyelashes. Most people do. Without a microscope you wouldn't find these hair follicle mites called Demodex that burrow into the base of a hair and feed on living tissue and dead skin cells. Neither would you see Entamoeba gingivalis, the parasitic amoebas that invade pockets in the gums around the base of your teeth, nor the bacteria called *Esherichia coli (E. coli)* that live in everyone's intestines. Disgusting as it may seem, we are their hosts. And like all good hosts, we provide the food and a safe place in which to eat it.

A parasite is usually defined as any organism that lives in or on another organism, called the host, and that takes nourishment from that host. The word *parasite* comes from an ancient Greek word that literally means "a person who sat down to dinner uninvited." These uninvited guests are not rare. They are so common, in fact, that there are more parasites than free-living creatures. Almost every plant and animal, including humans, plays host to one or more kinds of parasites during their lifetime. Parasites even have parasites, which are called hyperparasites. The one-celled parasite living in the digestive tract of a flea that lives on a dog is a hyperparasite.

Parasitism is one of several kinds of partnerships between species. As a group, these partnerships are described as symbiosis, which means "living together." When both partners mutually benefit from a symbiotic relationship, it is called mutualism. Termites and protozoans are mutual partners. Termites chew wood and swallow it, but they cannot digest the cellulose in it. Only the one-celled protozoans that live in the termite's gut have the right enzymes

*A termite emerging from its nest. Termites usually eat only the softer parts of wood, leaving the harder parts behind. Inset: A protozoan that lives in a termite's gut. Bacteria in the protozoan digest the cellulose in wood the termite eats.*

to break down the cellulose in wood and turn it into a sub-stance that can be digested by both the termites and proto-zoans. Each species of termite has its own kind of protozoan partner living in its gut that is so specific that scientists can tell the kind of termite just by knowing the protozoan that lives in its gut.

Cows and other grazing animals have similar mutual protozoan partners. When a cow swallows grass, it goes into the first stomach, called the rumen, where bacteria and other protozoans break down the cellulose in the grass. The proto-zoans in a cow's stomach only live about 20 hours, but they are quickly replaced by new generations. In exchange for their work, these protozoans get free food and a safe, warm place to live.

Ordinarily our relationship with the *E. coli* bacteria in our intestines is mutual. The bacteria go about their business of producing vitamin K, which we need for blood clotting. But if *E. coli* leave their usual intestinal habitat, they can quickly become parasitic. When human waste gets into a water sup-ply or contaminates food, *E. coli* can become a terrible villain. In the summer of 1993, the Centers for Disease Control (CDC) reported many cases of *E. coli* poisoning caused by people eating contaminated undercooked meat at fast-food restaurants. People who handle raw meat after they've used the bathroom without washing their hands thoroughly after-ward can spread *E. coli.*

A parasite lives inside or on its host for some part of its life. It is usually smaller than its host, and although it may harm its host, the parasite must never kill its host outright. The parasite must play a careful game. It is successful only if it keeps its host alive. If the host dies before the parasite can find another place to live, the parasite dies, too.

Even though a parasite gets an unlimited supply of food from its host, it faces hazards in each new habitat. A parasite that is swallowed by a warm-blooded animal, for example, must be able to survive the action of enzymes and hydrochloric acid in the host's stomach. A parasite can't thermoregulate, which means it cannot change, or regulate, its own body temperature. If it can't adapt to the host's temperature, the parasite must move to a more livable habitat, or it will die.

Whenever a parasite acts, the host reacts, back and forth, over and over, until they find a balance in which both can live. For example, when the parasitic trichina worm burrows into a person's muscle, that section of muscle fiber no longer works as a muscle. The host's body adapts to the invasion of the trichina worm by walling off that section of muscle into a kind of room, which keeps the parasite isolated. In reacting to different parasites, this walling off can occur in the liver, heart, brain, or other organs of the host.

The well-adapted host must get used to the invasion of a parasite, and a well-adapted parasite must get used to the host. Sometimes this action and reaction causes a change in color, size, or behavior of the host. Snails that are invaded by the larvae of a parasite called a fluke often grow larger than snails that do not have parasites. Potato plants that harbor tiny parasitic eelworms get bigger than potatoes without eelworms.

If you wander through a field in autumn you'll find hard, round bumps on dry stalks of goldenrod that look as though someone had inflated tiny balloons inside the stem. The bumps are called galls. When the goldenrod gall moth lays her eggs in the plant stem, the plant responds to the invasion by walling off the parasite. Oak trees, rose bushes, and hundreds of other plants react to different parasitic insects, mites, and worms with galls of various shapes and sizes.

Another tiny parasitic worm causes an amazing reaction in its snail host. In order to finish its life cycle, this worm must get out of the snail and into a bird's digestive system. It

*Two goldenrod galls. As the larvae of the goldenrod gall moth hatch, the gall swells, producing the characteristic shape shown on the left.*

does this by invading the slender eyestalks of the host snail. The snail's eyestalks react to the invasion by swelling into thick, throbbing, brightly colored "worms" that look enough like caterpillars to fool any bird. When a bird swoops down to catch this juicy pair of "caterpillars," it swallows the parasitic worms, and that solves the parasite's transportation problem into its final host.

Pearls can be an oyster's response to a parasitic invasion. A tiny parasitic worm inside an oyster's shell is as irritating to the oyster as a grain of sand, but the oyster has no way of throwing out the invader. So the oyster's reaction is to cover over the worm with layers of silky white mother-of-pearl, which is the material that lines its shell. The more layers of mother-of-pearl covering the parasite, the larger and more valuable the resulting pearl. This is why large, expensive natural pearls have sometimes been called "nothing more than ornamental parasites."

All plants are attacked by some kind of parasite, be it a virus, bacterium, fungus, mite, worm, or insect. Plants have no need to be parasitic themselves because they make their own food. Only one plant is completely parasitic. It is a vine called dodder, which cannot make food because its scales contain no chlorophyll. As a dodder vine twines around a host plant, its rootlike organs penetrate the host plant and absorb food and water.

Mistletoe is a part-time parasite that gets support and nutrients from a host tree even though it has chlorophyll and can make its own food. Birds drop mistletoe seeds in trees. When the seeds begin to grow, the roots poke through the bark of the host tree. Oak, apple, poplar, willow, and other host trees that provide support for this part-time parasite are often deformed by the mistletoe growing on them.

But how do people get parasites? Even in this age of shiny clean bathrooms and sanitary kitchens, humans are invaded by roundworms, flatworms, amoebas, and many other parasites from infected water and food. People can also get parasites through a vector, or carrier, such as a fly or mosquito. Other parasites arrive through sexual contact with an infected person, and still others invade people's bodies through the nose and skin. Pinworm eggs, for example, can be inhaled in contaminated dust, and hookworms can be picked up on the feet when walking barefoot.

The *Journal of the American Medical Association* predicts that by the year 2025, about 8.3 billion people world-

*A dodder vine wrapped around a plant. The root and older part of the plant stem eventually die and break off, leaving the dodder vine free. Dodder vines destroy many clover, alfalfa, and flax plants.*

wide will be infected with some kind of parasitic disease. Parasites are spreading faster than ever before because more people than ever are traveling to foreign countries. During the 1970s, as relations between the United States and the former Soviet Union eased, more than 80,000 tourists from the United States visited the Soviet Union in any one year. And about two weeks after they returned home, about 25 percent of those travelers came down with diarrhea and abdominal pains. When 83 percent of the people in one tour group got sick, the disease was traced to an old hotel in Leningrad (now called St. Petersburg) where the plumbing was broken down. The tourists who got sick were those who drank the tap water and brushed their teeth with it, not knowing it was contaminated with microscopic parasites that live in sewage.

Microscopic parasites thrive in water supplies contaminated by sewage because they travel in a hard protective covering called a cyst. These cysts are not always destroyed by chlorine or sewage processing. When the Mississippi River overflowed its banks and flooded miles and miles of surrounding land in the summer of 1993, sewage drains also overflowed. The overflow spread contaminated, untreated sewage, which remained in wells and reservoirs long after the flood subsided. Safe in their cysts, microscopic parasites can survive for years, but they can be killed in boiling water, which is why people in flooded areas are always advised to boil their drinking water.

Parasites travel home with armed forces personnel returning from overseas and with immigrants arriving from regions in Asia, Africa, and other areas of the world where sanitation may be primitive or where parasites are common. After the Korean War in the 1950s, and the Vietnam War in the 1960s and 1970s, thousands of soldiers returned infected by a variety of parasites. After the Desert Storm troops returned from the Gulf War in 1992, many of the service peo-

*Distributing pure drinking water after the Mississippi River flooded a water treatment plant in July 1993. People were told not to drink tap water as a precaution against picking up parasites, bacteria, and other organisms that might cause diseases.*

ple were infected with a parasitic protozoan that was carried by sand flies.

The increasing use of day-care centers has spread parasites like wildfire. Little children dig in sand and dirt and then put their hands in their mouths. If one child in a sandbox has pinworms or other parasites, the eggs or larvae of those parasites may drop into the sand. The chances are good that other children playing in that sandbox will pick up the eggs or larvae. Adult workers in day-care centers also spread pinworms and other parasites if they change children's diapers and then fail to wash their hands thoroughly before they serve food.

People in the United States have more pets than ever before, with about 110 million dogs and cats now living in our homes. Sixty-five different parasites and their infectious diseases can be carried to humans by dogs and 39 can be carried by cats.

Tennis champion Martina Navratilova fell ill to a parasite called toxoplasmosis, which can be transmitted by cats. And in one of the most expensive ski resorts in the United States, contaminated well water caused an outbreak of a disease caused by a parasite called Giardia. Parasites are invaders with no respect for boundaries. Young or old, rich or poor, anyone can become a host.

Although parasites have been around since before humans appeared on earth, the scientific study of parasites, called parasitology, is relatively new. Around 300 B.C., the Greek philosopher Aristotle described pinworms and tapeworms. These large parasites are easy to see in their adult stages. But hundreds of years went by after Aristotle described the worms before anyone solved the mystery of where they came from and how they moved through their life cycles. Such discoveries had to wait for the invention of the microscope in the middle of the seventeenth century, and for scientists to accumulate more information in all fields of zoology, the science of studying animals and animal life.

One of the first well-known parasitologists was a Belgian scientist, Pierre-Joseph van Beneden. Beginning in 1845, he worked for 15 years to unravel the life cycle of the tapeworm, particularly in fish. In 1875, he described his findings in his textbook *Commensals and Parasites in the Animal Kingdom.*

A German zoologist, Karl Rudolf Leuckart, is some-times called the founder of the modern science of parasitology because he was the first person to show that some human diseases, such as trichinosis, are caused by parasites. In his two-volume text *The Parasites of Man,* which was pub-

*Karl Rudolf Leuckart. In addition to showing that human diseases such as trichinosis are caused by wormlike parasites, Leuckart described the complicated life histories of various parasites, including tapeworms and flukes.*

lished in 1886, Leuckart explained how these parasitic invaders caused their damage.

Today, parasitologists work with electron microscopes and other modern technology. They do their research in many fields, including agriculture, veterinary medicine, botany, and entomology (the study of insects). But the area of many scientists' special interest is human medicine, where there is still a lot to be learned about the parasites that invade us.

# 2

# THE BLOODSUCKERS

Every once in a while, a big coho salmon is hauled out of Lake Erie wearing an ugly round scar on its side. The scar is caused by the largest parasite—the long, eellike sea lamprey that attaches itself to fish. The lamprey is related to an armored fish that lived millions of years ago. It has no bones, scales, or fins. And instead of jaws, the lamprey's mouth is a round suction disk centered by a tongue full of scrapers. This disk is so strong that a lamprey can use it to pull itself up the straight, wet wall of a canal. Ships are sometimes seen in the St. Lawrence River with lampreys two feet (61 centimeters) long clinging to their metal hulls. When a lamprey attaches its disk to a fish, it easily scrapes a hole in the fish's skin and sucks out the blood.

Sea lampreys must move into freshwater to lay their eggs. In spawning season, American sea lampreys swim from the Atlantic Ocean, through the St. Lawrence River, and into Lake Ontario. They never used to go into the other Great Lakes because they couldn't get past the barrier of Niagara Falls. But in 1829, the first Welland Canal was opened between Lake Ontario and Lake Erie. It was only 8 feet (2.4 meters) deep, but it was large enough to carry the ships in

*A lamprey, or jawless fish. The lamprey acts as a predator as well as a parasite. It feeds by clamping its mouth onto a live fish, boring a hole in its prey, and then sucking nutrients from the prey's blood.*

use at the time past the falls, and the lampreys followed. Then in 1912, the canal was extended and deepened to accommodate larger freighters. These conditions made it even easier for lampreys to become established in the other lakes. By the mid-1900s, lampreys had destroyed so many lake trout, whitefish, yellow pike, and blue pike that both sport fishing and the commercial fishing industry in the Great Lakes were just about ruined.

Lampreys are ectoparasites—they live outside their hosts. When conservationists from the United States and Canada studied the life cycle of these big ectoparasites, they found a way to control them. First they tried using electrified wire fences, called weirs, placed across the mouths of streams where lampreys spawned. A lot of lampreys were trapped by or turned away at the weirs, but many others made it through. The females continued to lay up to 100,000 eggs, which easily drifted through the wire barriers. After searching for other ways to control lampreys, scientists finally found a combination of chemicals that kills only the larvae of the lampreys without killing any fish. Since then, the Great Lakes have been stocked with chinook and coho salmon and several kinds of trout. Even though the fishing is good again, the chemical treatments will be continued until 1996 or beyond to make sure the lampreys don't become a big threat to fish again.

Leeches are considerably smaller than lampreys, but they are just as hungry for blood. If you had lived 1,000 years ago, a healer might have put a pair of two-inch- (five-centimeter- ) long leeches on your forehead to cure a headache. For many centuries, leeches were part of any doctor's equipment. Patients were bled for a variety of ailments ranging from fevers to tumors. In the 1920s and 1930s, anyone could go to a drugstore, pick out a leech from a jar on the

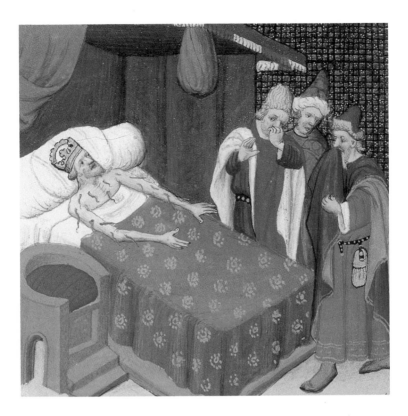

*Medicinal leeches being used in the treatment of disease. The patient is shown with numerous leeches on his body, which were hoped to cure him of a stomach ailment.*

shelf, rent it for 25 cents, and use it to draw blood from a black eye or other bruise.

When a medicinal leech feeds, it presses its three razor-sharp jaws against the patient's skin and cuts through it like a circular saw, leaving a *Y*-shaped wound. Sometimes this leeching treatment worked, although no one knew how or why. Now we know that a leech's salivary glands produce a substance called hirudin, which numbs the wound and keeps the blood from clotting. A single leech can suck up about a tablespoon of blood before it feels full and drops off, but an equal amount of blood will continue to flow before it clots.

Leeches are still sometimes used to treat black-and-blue bruises, especially around the eyes, or to reduce blood pressure wherever blood accumulates when circulation is poor. But the major use of leeches today is as a source of a drug that helps heart attack victims. A substance called hematin is extracted from the hirudin collected from giant Amazon leeches that are raised on leech farms for medical purposes. Hematin dissolves blood clots after they form. It can actually stop the progress of a heart attack by dissolving the clots that are preventing blood from flowing through the heart during an attack. In this way, the clots are prevented from doing more damage.

Leeches are little more than tubes an inch or two (2.5 or 5 centimeters) long, with suckers at either end. The rear end hangs on to the host while the mouth end sucks blood. One scientist has said that the leech would be the perfect astronaut for long space flights because it is probably the only animal that doesn't seem to suffer from hunger. Once it has filled its stretchable body cavity with blood, it can take six months to digest the meal. This is possible because bacteria in the leech's gut prevent the stored blood from decaying.

Duck leeches get into the mouths and nasal passages of waterfowl. Fish leeches attach themselves to the gills of fish, where they can gorge themselves on freshly oxygenated blood. A bird or fish host can survive a few of these parasites, but too many leeches can cause a bird to suffocate or a fish to die from loss of blood.

The horse leech lives in creeks, ponds, and other freshwater. When horses and cattle drink from leech-infested water, the leeches crawl into their nostrils and down into their throats. As the leeches drink blood, the horses' or cattle's throat tissues swell, and these big animals can choke to death if they don't get help in time.

Leeches that live in freshwater also prey on people. Some kinds can enter through any body opening when a person is swimming or washing in the leech-infested streams or lakes found in parts of Africa, southern Europe, and the Near East. Other kinds of water leeches enter the body in drinking water and attach themselves to the lining of the victim's throat, where they are easily inhaled into the lungs. A person

*A parasitic pond leech. Some parasitic leeches use bladelike jaws to cut the skin of their hosts, whereas others secrete enzymes that digest a hole through their hosts' skin.*

can survive one or two of these parasites, but anyone who is host to several of these leeches can die of infection, suffocation, or anemia caused by the loss of blood.

Land leeches that live in southeastern Asia and South America are dangerous to humans, too. Even when people wear protective clothing, these leeches crawl through buttonholes or small rips in clothing. Because hirudin numbs the cut from the leech's sharp jaws, it is not unusual for people to say they didn't even know the leech was on them until they saw blood flowing from the wound. People working in a field infested with huge numbers of these leeches can suffer severe blood loss before realizing they've played host to these parasites.

Ticks are the bloodsuckers to watch out for in North America, especially in summer and early fall when people go walking in wooded areas. Ticks are eight-legged animals called arachnids, close cousins of spiders. When a tick lands on a person, it pierces the skin and drives in a hollow tube that works like a straw. Then the tick's head burrows in, and the tick hangs on as long as it is drinking blood, which might be anywhere from five days to two weeks if no one notices it. The big danger from ticks is disease because they are notorious carriers as well as parasites. Different kinds of ticks carry the organisms that cause diseases such as Rocky Mountain spotted fever, Lyme disease, Texas cattle fever, and tularemia (rabbit fever).

Mites are similar to ticks, but much smaller. Some are microscopic. No matter what their size, all mites are irritating. The itch mite, with the scientific name Sarcoptes scabiei, is one of the tiniest mites. It has the honor of being the first organism positively identified as the cause of a specific human disease by an Italian physician, Giovanni Bonomo. That was in 1687, when the disease was given the name sca-

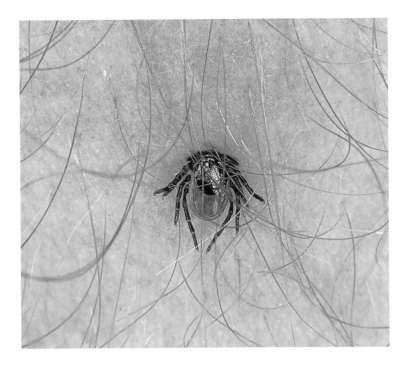

*A tick feeding on human blood. During its life cycle, a tick feeds just three times—as a larva, a nymph, and an adult. It is the nymph that usually feeds on humans.*

bies. The itch mite causes a lot of misery as it tunnels under skin, causing a rash and itchiness. A slightly different kind of scabies can be transmitted to people by dogs that carry the dog itch mite.

The vampire bat isn't usually found on lists of parasites, but it is the only mammal that lives on the blood of another living animal. Despite what we sometimes see in horror movies, the common vampire bats found in Mexico and South America are not very big, only two or three inches (five to eight centimeters) long. They fly from their roosts at dusk in search of any warm-blooded animals, often settling on cows, horses, or pigs. The host may not even feel the bat as it lands, or the bite of the bat's razor-sharp teeth. The bat does not suck the blood from the wound. Instead, the bat laps up the blood with its tongue. It's not the bite or loss of blood that causes farmers to worry about their animals. What they fear is the threat of rabies, which is spread by infected mammals, including bats. Rabies is a deadly, incurable disease caused by a virus that attacks an animal's central nervous system. A person who handles an animal with rabies can easily pick up this virus through an open sore or a small cut.

# 3

# FLATWORMS AND ROUNDWORMS

Flukes are parasitic flatworms, and each kind of fluke has a specific host. But otherwise, all flukes have the same basic life cycle, with a snail as the intermediate host. Only a few species of snails can be this go-between host, however, and most of those snails live in the tropics. In order to be invaded by a parasitic fluke, a person has to be in water where both the fluke and the snail live.

There are no native blood flukes that parasitize humans in the United States or Canada, but there are flukes that parasitize water birds and mammals such as muskrats. Swimmer's itch is a disease caused by the larva of freshwater flukes that swim around in lakes or ponds looking for a bird or muskrat. If these flukes make the mistake of burrowing into the skin of a human swimmer, they're in for a big surprise. The human host is a dead end, and life is soon over for these larvae because they are not equipped to survive in the habitat of a human host. The human victim of this mistaken invasion is left for a while with an itchy rash where the fluke larvae tunneled into the skin.

At the seashore, another species of fluke causes clam digger's itch, or sea itch. Children are more likely than adults to get this annoying rash because they dash in and out of the water without drying off. But if you rub your skin with a towel as soon as you leave the water, the tiny larvae will rub off, too.

Other flukes are not that easy to get rid of. In fact, the World Health Organization says that flukes are one of the world's major health problems because flukes live in every kind of vertebrate animal. And flukes have been with us for a long time. Some fluke eggs were found in a 2,000-year-old Egyptian mummy, and flukes were probably around long before that time.

Most flukes are less than an inch long. Some are ectoparasites, while others are endoparasites that live inside their hosts. Most flukes have complicated life cycles that involve several hosts. Although adult flukes can live in a wide variety of environments, the eggs of most flukes must hatch in water. After hatching, the larvae swim around until they find their first host, a snail. The larvae have only about 24 hours to get into the right snail or the larvae will die. Scientists say that when a fluke larva senses a nearby snail, it races straight toward it "like iron filings to a magnet."

Once inside the snail, the larvae produce little sacs called sporocysts that bud into another kind of larvae called cercaria. Cercaria look like miniature tadpoles as they swim about waiting to bore into or be swallowed by their final host. Hundreds of thousands of sporocysts and cercaria come from only one larva that hatched from one egg. This means that a single egg can infect hundreds of thousands of hosts, and that egg is only one of millions from one adult fluke. No wonder 250 million people are parasitized by flukes! On the other hand, some parasitologists think it's a wonder more people don't have flukes.

Three blood flukes called schistosomes are major parasites that cause serious problems for people, especially in regions where sanitation systems are poor or don't exist at all. Schistosome blood flukes are most common in parts of Asia, Africa, the Middle East, South America, and the Caribbean Islands.

Blood flukes are odd little worms that mate for life, which can be as long as 30 years. The male, which is less than an inch long, has a grooved canal the length of its underside, where the female settles in for this long "marriage." The flukes' habitat is a human vein around the

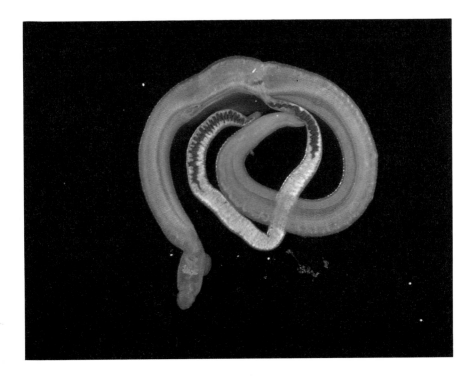

*Adult intestinal blood flukes that cause schistosomiasis. The thick, blue male and threadlike, white female normally live in pairs in blood vessels of the small intestine. Humans become infected while bathing or working in water contaminated by these worms.*

intestines or bladder, where the male worm hangs on with suckers at its head end.

The female churns out about 3,500 microscopic eggs a day in a small blood vessel. When it gets clogged with eggs, the blood vessel ruptures. The eggs spill into the host's intestines and travel out of the host with the feces. If the eggs land in a toilet, that's the end of them. But in areas where human waste, called night soil, is used to fertilize the ground, the eggs find the right moist, warm conditions that allow them to survive and hatch.

Some blood fluke eggs also hatch in irrigation ditches, rice paddies, and ponds, where the larvae begin their search for snails to burrow into. After they have fed on the snails' tissues, the larvae have changed and are ready to move on again. At this stage they have grown a pair of suckers that help them latch onto a human host who happens to be standing in the water. When larvae burrow into this new host's skin, they first get into tiny capillaries. Then they move into larger veins until they reach the heart and eventually the lungs. From there the larvae go to the blood vessels around the liver. They stay there for about three weeks, feeding on rich blood and growing fast. When the fluke larvae become adult worms, they start their final journey. They swim upstream against the flow of blood and land in the small vessels around the intestines or bladder. And there the worms may lead a comfortable life for the lifetime of the host.

This infestation of worms is not so comfortable for the host, of course. Schistosomiasis, the disease caused by these worms, starts with the misery of skin irritation as the fluke larvae burrow in. When the parasites reach the lungs, the person develops pneumonialike symptoms. These symptoms are followed by the most devastating part of the disease: the victim cannot breathe easily with lungs full of parasites, and eventually the person grows too weak to work. Sadly, this disease thrives among the poorest people of the world, many of whom may already be suffering from the weakness caused by malnutrition.

Knowing that night soil contains parasites, it may seem strange that people continue to use it. But in poor, heavily populated countries, people can seldom afford other fertilizers. Night soil costs nothing, is rich in nitrogen, and has kept the soil fertile enough to be cultivated for thousands of years. Technology doesn't always make life better for people in poor countries either. Sometimes it favors the parasite. When the Aswan High Dam was built on the Nile River to bring hydroelectric power to Egypt, it also brought an enormous increase in blood flukes. As irrigation ditches were dug across the country, wonderful new habitats for snails were created. The Upper Volta Dam did the same thing in Africa. Areas where few blood flukes had lived before were turned into huge reservoirs for these parasites.

The tapeworm is another notorious endoparasite. More than 3,000 species of tapeworms exist, and they live in almost every species of vertebrate. The tapeworm is a long, gutless flatworm with no digestive system, no respiratory system, and no circulatory system. In other words, it cannot digest food, it cannot breathe on its own, and it does not have a blood supply. It lives by soaking up digested food from its host. Its head, called the scolex, has no eyes, mouth, nose, or ears. There is a bit of nerve tissue in the head that might loosely be called a brain, but the only function of the head is to find a place in the host's intestine to hook on to. The beef tapeworm has sucker disks on its head, but the pork tapeworm is doubly secure. It also has hooks that keep it anchored against the constant flow of digested food passing by.

*Aswan High Dam, Egypt. Building the dam provided an enlarged habitat for snails, and people living near the dam suffered an enormous increase in infection by Schistosoma blood flukes. Today, hope for wiping out the disease lies with the development of a vaccine.*

All the segments of a tapeworm's body grow from the scolex. The segment closest to the head is the youngest, and those farthest from the head are mature adults. A tapeworm that has lived in a person for several years may be 40 feet (12 meters) long and have more than 3,000 segments. Each segment contains both male and female organs. The adult segments at the end of the tapeworm are each filled with as many as 100,000 eggs. When the eggs are ripe, the segment at the end of the tapeworm ruptures, and the eggs move out of the intestines and out of the body with the feces.

But before a tapeworm can fully develop, it needs an intermediate host. It gets to that host when animals feed where infected human waste has been deposited. If a cow eats the grass where tapeworm eggs have been deposited, it swallows some eggs, which then hatch in the cow's digestive tract. Larvae that survive this far and are not carried out with cow's feces, bore through the animal's intestinal wall and into a blood vessel. From there the larvae are carried by the bloodstream to the cow's muscles, where they form a capsule, or cyst, about the size of a jelly bean. If meat from that cow is well-cooked, the cyst is destroyed and that's the end of the tapeworm. A person can even swallow the eggs of a beef tapeworm and nothing will happen because the eggs are killed by the stomach's digestive enzymes. But if a person swallows the cyst of a tapeworm in undercooked or raw meat, the tapeworm comes out of its cyst, attaches its head to the intestinal wall, and settles down to live in its human host.

Usually only one beef tapeworm at a time infects a person. Pork tapeworms are much more dangerous because many larval cysts are likely to be swallowed in an undercooked piece of pork. The pork tapeworm larvae work their way into the nervous system, the brain, and other organs before one finally anchors itself in the small intestine. A larval cyst in the brain can destroy nerve cells, which cannot repair themselves. It can also cause a person to have seizures that are sometimes mistaken for epilepsy, a disorder that also causes seizures.

In his book *New Guinea Tapeworms and Jewish*

*Grandmothers, Tales of Parasites and People,* Dr. Robert Desowitz says that parasites are often connected to the habits of different cultures. Some groups of people never eat pork, so they aren't exposed to pork parasites. But the pig is vital to the lives of some other groups of people. In New Guinea, for example, pork is so important that the people are almost continually infected with pork parasites.

Also in his book, Dr. Desowitz describes a 1930s New York City mystery that puzzled doctors until they figured out the cultural connection. It seems that among a population of elderly Jewish women, who follow rigid standards of food cleanliness, doctors were finding many who were infected

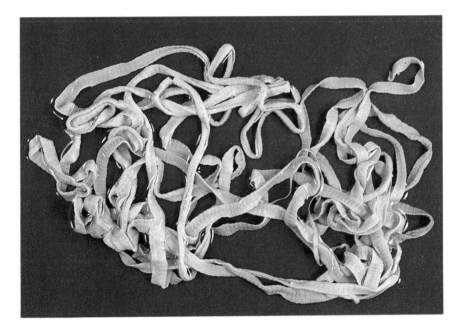

*Part of a fish tapeworm. The scolex has a combination of hooks and suckers that keeps the worm from being swept away by traffic in the intestine. Some drugs that are effective against tapeworms make the worms so sick the scolex lets go.*

with tapeworms. The source of these tapeworm infections was finally traced back to Scandinavian fishermen.

The fish tapeworms first came to the United States in the late 1800s when infected Scandinavian fishermen settled around the lakes of Minnesota and Wisconsin. There wasn't any indoor plumbing on their fishing boats, so the fishermen used the lakes as their bathrooms. When the fish tapeworm eggs were released in the human waste, they were eaten by the larvae of clams, barnacles, and other crustaceans in the water. Next, fish ate the crustaceans that had eaten the eggs, and the eggs hatched into larvae that settled in the muscles of the fish. It wasn't long before fish in the lakes were carrying tapeworm larvae.

Many of the infected fish were sent to markets in New York City. Among other shoppers, Jewish women bought these fresh fish to make gefilte fish, which are dumplings of minced fish that are dropped into water and boiled until done. Dr. Desowitz says the "until done" part was the tricky part. In the 1930s, good cooks didn't use gadgets such as cooking thermometers to see if food was cooked enough. What they did was taste-test their recipes. In the case of gefilte fish, the first samples the cooks tasted were still fairly raw, and any tapeworm larvae in the food would have still been alive. "In this way," says Dr. Desowitz, "many a nice old lady . . . unwittingly acquired a 40-foot Scandinavian immigrant in her digestive tract."

Today, even if cooks sample the food they are cooking when it is still almost raw, they are unlikely to get fish tapeworms. Fish tapeworms are rare now because fish are inspected for parasites and fishing boats have bathrooms and other sanitary facilities on board.

Roundworms are parasites with an unfavorable reputation similar to that of flatworms. The world teems with some 12,000 different kinds of roundworms, and there are billions of each kind. It has been said that if you dig up a shovelful of soil, it would contain a million roundworms, many of which feed on plants. And of the thousands of kinds of roundworms, about 50 species infect humans. All these parasites are cylindrical worms with pointed ends that look like wriggly white sewing thread. A hard covering called a cuticle protects these worms in all kinds of habitats.

Ascaris is the largest roundworm, ranging from a few inches to a foot long. It looks a lot like an earthworm. It has a simple life cycle, and it infects about 650 million people worldwide. The female Ascaris may lay as many as 200,000 eggs a day in the intestines of its host, usually a pig, horse, or person. The eggs pass out of the host in the feces. When they land on the ground, the eggs can survive for five years or more because their shells are so tough they can withstand all kinds of conditions, and a number of poisonous chemicals. But the eggs cannot develop any further until they are swallowed by another host, which could be a person or a large animal. A person may pick up Ascaris eggs by eating unwashed vegetables grown in contaminated soil. The eggs hatch in the host's intestine and begin to tour the body. During this trip through the body, Ascaris causes the most damage. At first, when the worms burrow through the intestinal wall into blood vessels, the host may experience mild stomach pains and diarrhea. The worms then continue to move in and out of various organs until they reach the lungs. In the lungs the worms cause asthmalike wheezing, congestion, and coughing. When the worms move into the throat, they are swallowed back into the intestines. There they feed on digested food and produce eggs, which start the whole cycle again. Ascaris worms lodged in the intestines can cause such violent abdominal pains that the attack is sometimes mistaken for a bleeding ulcer or appendicitis.

Pinworms are such common parasites that most

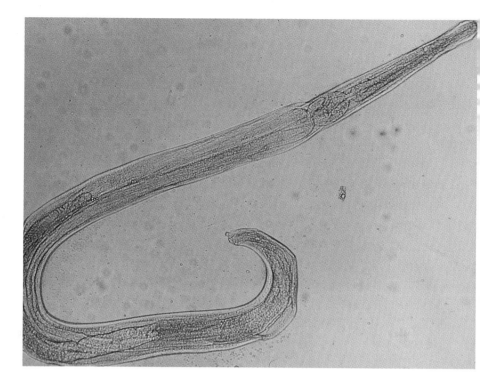

*A pinworm, one of the most common roundworms in humans. The worm has a tube-within-a-tube body plan. The digestive tract is the inner tube within the rest of the animal, which is the transparent outer tube.*

people have them at some time during their life, usually as a child. These little white roundworms live in the intestines, where they usually cause mild discomfort. In extreme cases, however, they can cause convulsions. Pinworms are most irritating at night, when the female worms crawl out of the host's rectum to lay eggs. Little children are likely to scratch in their sleep and pick up the eggs on their fingers. Then, if they suck their thumbs, the eggs are swallowed, and the process repeats itself.

Pinworms and eggs can spread quickly through a family on towels, bedding, toys, dishes, and toilet seats. They can be inhaled in house dust. Pinworms can also be spread in water. A person can get pinworms just by sitting in a bathtub previously used by someone who has pinworms. The quick cure for pinworms is an effective medication prescribed by a doctor, but pinworms can be prevented if people wash their hands thoroughly and often, especially after going to the bathroom.

Before indoor bathrooms were installed in homes, hookworms were very common, especially in warm climates. These threadlike worms are still common today in poor areas where the bathroom may be an outhouse or simply the outdoors. World health officials estimate that about 450 million people worldwide are infected with hookworms. Anyone who walks barefoot on moist ground that is contaminated by human waste can pick up hookworm larvae on their feet. The worms burrow into the skin through hair follicles and sweat glands. Then they move into blood vessels and are carried to the lungs. From there the hookworms move into the throat. They are swallowed and, like Ascaris worms, they settle in their last habitat, the small intestine. The hookworms' trip through the body to the small intestine takes about seven weeks, but they may stay in the host for up to 15 years. When hookworms are in a person's lungs, they cause fever and coughing. By the time they are feeding on blood in the intestines, the worms have caused anemia and general weakness that often leaves people unable to fight off other diseases. Hookworms may also be to blame for the reputation many poor people in hot, moist climates have for being slow and lazy. In addition to being undernourished, these people have no energy because they are constantly infected with hookworms.

Trichina is the only roundworm that isn't spread in con-

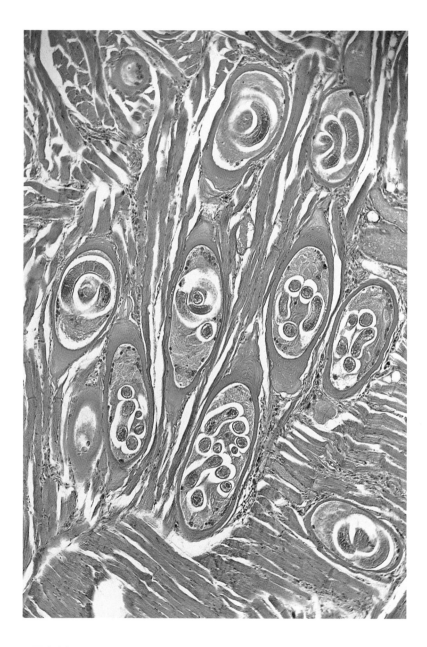

*Trichina worm cysts in pork. In humans, the worms cause trichinosis. The encysted worms were first discovered in 1835 by a British medical student while he was dissecting a cadaver.*

taminated soil. It arrives in the human body by way of meat, particularly pork. Although trichina cysts are also found in the muscles of bears and walruses, not many people in the United States eat bear or walrus. But anyone who eats under-cooked pork has a good chance of swallowing the cysts of these tiny, spiral-shaped worms. The hard coating of the cysts dissolves in the intestine, which frees the tiny larvae and allows them to burrow into the intestinal wall. From there they enter blood vessels that carry them to all parts of the body. Most often the larvae settle in muscles in the arms, chest, larynx, jaws, tongue, eyes, and diaphragm, where they can stay alive for many years in their hard capsules. Trichinosis is the name given to the disorder caused by an infestation of these parasites. Doctors say it is difficult to diagnose trichinosis because the symptoms may seem like the flu or 50 other diseases, depending on where the para-sites have settled. As the trichina cysts get harder, or calcify, they cause pain, stiffness, and swelling, which can be relieved with anti-inflammatory drugs. While the parasites are still in a person's intestines, they can be destroyed with a drug called thiabendazole. Because large-scale inspections of pork aren't reliable in finding trichina, the best safeguard is to cook pork thoroughly before eating it.

# 4

# MICROSCOPIC PARASITES

When Antonie van Leeuwenhoek built his first simple micro-scopes 300 years ago in his small shop in Amsterdam, the lenses were so precisely ground that lens makers today still cannot understand how he made lenses with such clarity using the equipment available to him then. Van Leeuwenhoek wasn't a trained scientist, but in his notes he described the "wee beasties" and "tiny animacules" he saw with his microscopes. Scientists today believe what van Leeuwenhoek saw was probably Giardia, a one-celled organism, or protozoan, that propels itself along with eight little whiplike tails called flagella. Giardia has two nuclei that make it look like a tiny clown face, but there is nothing funny about this parasite that infects millions of people.

One of the secrets of Giardia's success is its cyst. The cyst covers Giardia so securely that it can stay dormant for months, even on trips through sewage-processing stations. This is the parasite that often comes home from foreign lands with travelers, leaving them with abdominal pains, diarrhea, and nausea for weeks. Giardia spreads from unwashed hands to mouth, in contaminated water, and on unwashed salad greens. It is not even safe to drink from a crystal clear mountain stream because it may be contaminated by the

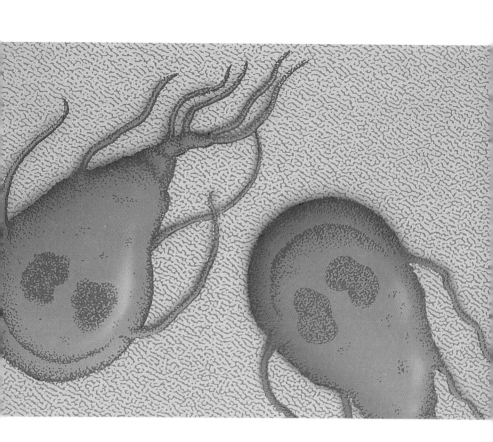

*Giardia, showing its two nuclei and eight flagella. Giardia attach to the intestinal wall by means of adhesive disks, but they do not always produce symptoms because the cells of the intestine are replaced every three to four days.*

feces of muskrats, bears, raccoons, and other wild animals that commonly carry Giardia. Reservoirs that get their water from contaminated streams may spread these parasites to city dwellers, even though the water is treated before it reaches the users' faucets. At one time giardiasis was called "beaver fever" because it was thought that only beavers carried Giardia cysts. But now we know that pets such as dogs, cats, and parakeets also carry the parasite. Flies that stomp around in filth pick up Giardia and leave the parasites at their next landing site, which could be the snack you are enjoying outdoors on a nice day. Fortunately, giardiasis is easily treated with a prescription antibiotic.

Another one-celled parasite that moves around by means of flagella is trypanosome, which causes African sleeping sickness. The carrier of trypanosome is the tsetse fly, and the main host for the parasite is a human. But the intermediate host, known as the reservoir, may be a cow, an antelope, or some other large animal. All three of these—carrier, reservoir, and host—must be available to trypanosome in order for it to spread its terrible disease. If the tsetse fly bites and drinks the blood of an infected antelope, it also drinks in the trypanosomes with the blood. When the infected tsetse fly bites a person, the trypanosomes get into the person's blood through the wound. Trypanosomes can stay in the host's bloodstream for weeks or years before they move into the lymph glands. From there they move into the nervous system, especially the brain and spinal cord, where they do the most damage. Sleeping sickness is a long-lasting disease that weakens the victim and results in extreme sleepiness. Many people die from this disease each year in Africa.

Amoebas are one-celled animals that ooze along on "false feet" called pseudopods, looking for food to engulf. Many amoebas are harmless, but one called Entamoeba histolytica is an out-and-out villain. This parasite is protected in a cyst as it spreads dysentery, a disease that causes severe abdominal pain, fever, and bloody diarrhea. Dysentery is most commonly passed along by an infected person who handles food with unwashed hands, and often this carrier doesn't even show any symptoms of the disease. But dysentery is also common in hot, humid, tropical regions, especially where people are crowded together in places with no sewage treatment or sanitary bathrooms. The disease can spread like wildfire through crowded prisoner-of-war camps and temporary shelters set up quickly after a major disaster.

Plasmodium is an ancient enemy. It is a protozoan that does not have flagella or pseudopods. It is simply carried along in the bloodstream of its host. In different places and in different centuries, the disease this parasite carries has been known as chills and fever, ague, miasmic fever, marsh fever, blackwater fever, and coastal fever. We know it as malaria, the disease that has killed more people than all wars combined. The malaria plasmodium is carried by the female *Anopheles*

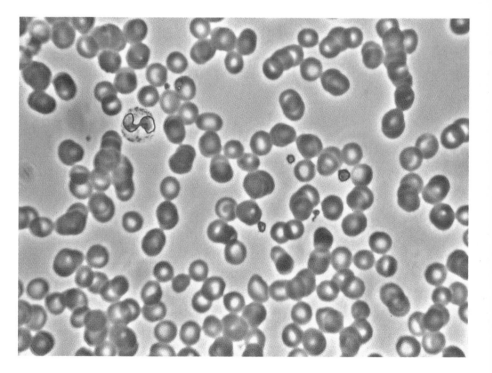

*The malaria parasite, plasmodium. The infected red blood cell shows the characteristic dumbbell shape of the parasite at this stage in its life cycle. When infected cells are destroyed, the victim develops anemia and fever.*

mosquito. Both male and female *Anopheles* mosquitoes drink nectar and plant juices, but the female needs a meal of blood before she can lay her eggs. If she bites a person who has malaria, she takes in the plasmodium spores with the drink of blood. When the infected mosquito bites the next person, the spores are passed along with the mosquito's saliva into the bite. The spores travel in the bloodstream to the new human host's liver, where they invade the red blood cells. One of the symptoms of malaria is chills and fever that comes in cycles every 48 to 72 hours. The fever is a reaction to the spores periodically breaking out of the blood cells and sending poisons into the bloodstream.

Malaria has been controlled in humans by quinine and other drugs that act on the parasite at different stages of its life cycle. The spread of the disease has also been controlled by insecticides that kill the mosquitoes, but scientists have reported that both the mosquitoes and the parasites are developing resistance to these chemicals. The best hope of wiping out malaria seems to be in finding a vaccine against it. Scientists have developed techniques to grow the parasite in a laboratory, which is the first step toward creating such a vaccine.

A killer disease called kala-azar, or leishmaniasis, is as old as malaria, but it was seldom heard of in this country until troops from the United States fought in the Gulf War in 1991. Kala-azar is caused by a one-celled parasite called Leishmania, and it is carried by tiny sand flies found in Africa, Asia, Latin America, and the Middle East. People get the parasite when they are bitten by infected sand flies. About two months after being bitten, an infected person develops a fever and anemia that gradually worsen. In 95 percent of cases that go untreated, the victims die. Fortunately, the U.S. service people who were infected with kala-azar were treated with drugs that kill the parasite. But others were not so lucky. One medical relief worker for the United Nations told a reporter about whole families and villages wiped out by kala-azar in 1993, when 60,000 people in southern Sudan were cut off from medical help during a civil war there.

Viruses are the smallest known parasites. They can only be seen with an electron microscope. Smallpox and rabies are caused by viruses. The discovery of vaccines for both these diseases seems quite miraculous because the vaccines were developed long before anyone had seen either virus with an electron microscope.

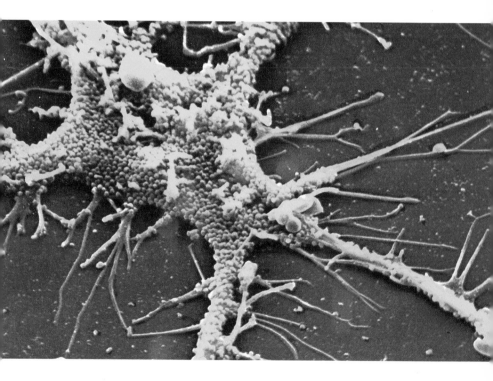

*A cell infected by a virus. The small, sphere-shaped virus particles cover the surface of the cell body and its limbs. This type of virus causes cold sores and the eye infection conjunctivitis in humans.*

Without a host, a virus seems lifeless. It is nothing more than a strand of genetic material inside a protein coat. But when a virus enters a living cell, it takes over and turns the cell into a virus-making machine. In addition to causing smallpox and rabies, viruses cause AIDS, colds, measles, chicken pox, whooping cough, polio, pneumonia, some cancers, and enough other diseases to make viruses enemy number one on any list of parasites. The study of this enormous group of parasites is called virology.

A fungus has no way to make its own food, like a plant, and it has no mouth to take in food, like an animal. A fungus absorbs food through its thin cell wall. When fungi absorb their food from dead matter, they act as decomposers and are part of the necessary process of decay. But when fungi take their food from living plants and animals, they are parasites.

Yeasts, molds, mildews, smuts, and slime molds are some of the parasitic fungi that attack plants and cause dozens of diseases, such as corn smut, Dutch elm disease, chestnut blight, grape mildew, and potato blight. Between 1845 and 1851, millions of people in Ireland starved to death because the potato blight destroyed their one major crop, potatoes. With no way to stop the fungus, about a million and a half people left Ireland during the years of famine. Most of these people moved to the United States and Canada.

Ringworm is not a worm, but a fungus. It is the same parasitic fungus that causes athlete's foot. In both ringworm and athlete's foot, the host develops blisters and itchy, flaking skin. Athlete's foot is simply the name given to the disease when it is found on feet. When the disease appears on other parts of the body, it is called ringworm. This fungus is easily treated with medications that contain antifungal chemicals.

The resident parasitic bacteria that live constantly in our bodies are no danger to us unless they move to places where they don't belong. The bacteria in our mouths, for

*People attacking a potato store during the Irish potato famine. Potato blight made potatoes, which were the staple food of Ireland, so scarce that people fought for them.*

example, do little harm there. But if they move into the inner ear, the bacteria cause painful infections. *E. coli* bacteria are just fine if they stay put in our intestines. But if the bacteria move to the bladder or some other organ, they can cause serious infections.

Other bacteria are called opportunistic because they take advantage of opportunities to move into new habitats.

Bacteria commonly found in our throats are adapted to conditions there and so they don't bother us. But if a person's immune system runs down for some reason, or the person gets another disease that changes the body temperature and other conditions in the bacteria's usual habitat, the bacteria take the opportunity to move to the lungs. In the lungs, they can cause pneumonia. A similar situation develops in people with AIDS. These people seldom die of AIDS itself. Instead, diseases caused by bacteria, viruses, fungi, and other organisms that move in when the immune system is too weak to defend the body are often the cause of death.

# 5

# STRANGERS
# IN THE NEST

Most parasitism takes place between individual hosts and parasites, but sometimes whole societies of animals are involved. There are termites that have termites in their houses. Three different kinds of termites are host to another species of termite that lives in the walls of the host termite's nest and eats whatever the host provides.

Ants parasitize ants, too. Dr. Edward O. Wilson, who probably knows more about ants than anyone on earth, says that some ants have learned to "break the code" of other ant societies in order to get into their nests. According to Dr. Wilson, "The individual parasite species track down host colonies, gain acceptance as members, and persuade the workers to feed them."

Parasitic worker ants march out in columns and force their way into the nests of other species. These workers have strong jaws made for fighting. Once they are in a foreign nest, the workers take the developing ants, the pupae, in their jaws and carry them back to their own nests. When the pupae become adults, they also become slaves. The slave ants do all the work, while the worker ants stroke their backs. Doing this forces the slave ants to regurgitate food for the parasitic ants.

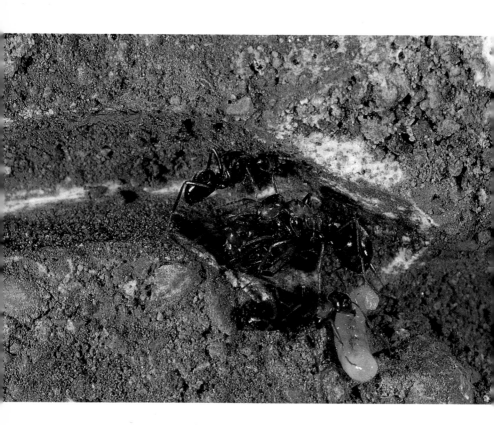

*Slave-making ants invading a colony of another species and carrying off a pupa. When stolen pupae become adults, they also become slaves, serving their captors and helping to increase their population.*

A bird that invades another bird's nest is called a brood parasite. There are about 80 species of birds that live like this. The female European cuckoo bird, for example, does not build a nest of her own. Instead, she flies over a large territory in search of one. But the cuckoo isn't looking for just any old empty nest. She needs one which has eggs in it that are being tended. If the cuckoo finds a nest she likes, but the eggs have already hatched, she destroys the young birds, usually by pushing them out of the nest. When any bird's eggs or young are destroyed, that bird will lay another clutch of eggs. So the cuckoo waits, and as soon as new eggs appear in the nest she wants to parasitize, the cuckoo adds her own eggs and flies off, never to see her eggs again. Her young will survive without her because the host bird will instinctively put food into the open mouths of all the baby birds in the nest. Scientists have found that a bird recognizes its newly hatched young only by their position in the nest, by the appearance of widely opened mouths, or by begging sounds. Dr. Wilson calls newly hatched birds "little more than helpless eating machines" which the parent or host bird keeps filling.

Cuckoo birds around the world have developed amazing ways to intimidate or trick host birds into accepting their eggs. Two kinds of hawk cuckoos in India, for example, mimic the coloring and flight of a sparrow hawk, which preys on smaller birds. When a hawk cuckoo makes a pass overhead, a small bird in a nest recognizes the flight pattern as that of the enemy sparrow hawk. If the small bird is frightened enough to leave its nest, the female hawk cuckoo moves in and deposits her eggs in the empty nest.

Another Indian cuckoo called the koel has a clever way of tricking a crow into leaving its nest. The male koel perches close to the crow's nest and squawks until it attracts the crow's attention. Then the male koel allows itself to be driven away by the crow. While the crow is off chasing the male, the female koel has time to lay her eggs in the abandoned crow's nest.

Parasitic birds also have other adaptations that help them live this kind of life. The female cuckoo has an egg-laying canal or tube, called the cloaca, that can be pushed out unusually far. The extended cloaca allows the cuckoo to drop eggs into nests built in crevices and holes that are too

*A reed warbler feeding a cuckoo. The absence of young warblers in the nest suggests that the larger cuckoo outcompeted the young warblers for space, food, and parental attention.*

small for her body. And the eggs of parasitic birds are specially adapted to give them a better chance of survival. The shell of the cuckoo's egg is thicker and stronger than those of its host, so if any egg is broken, it probably won't be one laid by the cuckoo.

The eggs of brood parasite birds tend to look like the eggs of the host birds. Dr. Wilson says this amazing mimicry of egg color and pattern is "a first-class scientific mystery." And because birds recognize eggs only by size and color, a parasitic bird can slip its look-alike eggs into a host nest unnoticed. In laboratory tests, most birds showed a preference for larger eggs with slightly different patterns than their own, so brood parasite eggs don't have to match exactly in order to be accepted by the host bird. European cuckoos have three main hosts for their eggs—a redstart, which lays unspotted blue eggs; a brambling, which lays pale blue eggs with reddish spots; and a pied wagtail, which lays white eggs flecked with gray. Yet the cuckoos are so host specific that their eggs mimic only those of the bird whose nest they have chosen to invade.

After the eggs hatch, the new young cuckoos carry on the battle for survival in the host nest. The first thing the young cuckoos do is to get rid of the eggs or babies of the host bird. The cuckoos simply shove them out of their own nest. Newly hatched honeyguide birds are especially good at this kind of push-and-shove because they have sharp hooks at the tips of their beaks that they use to pierce eggs and kill young host birds.

An altricial bird is one whose young are helpless at birth, and only birds with altricial young are victims of brood parasitism. Precocial birds seldom play host to parasites because a precocial bird is one that can take care of itself as soon as it hatches. Ducks, geese, and other precocial birds form a close attachment to their parents because they must follow the parents in order to find food. They aren't fed in the nest. This attachment, which is called imprinting, is such a basic instinct that a precocial bird will imprint on the first moving object it sees. Zookeepers and farmers know what it's like to become the "mother" to newly hatched goslings or chicks that follow them everywhere. The only precocial bird known to be parasitic is the South American black-headed duck, but it only stays in the nest of its host for a day or two before it goes off to live on its own.

Dr. Wilson has spent a large part of his life studying

*Canada geese imprinted to a human. Young birds that become imprinted to objects other than their mothers grow up preferring the objects, rather than their own species, as companions and mates.*

social parasitism, and he believes "the discoveries yet to be made will sustain our sense of wonder for a long time to come." This is probably true for all the kinds of parasitism that exist in nature.

Parasitism is really a special kind of ecology. As ecologists have learned, all organisms in a habitat are connected in a great web of interaction. If one kind of animal or plant is taken out of the web forever, the whole habitat adjusts in some way to the change. And so it is with parasites and their hosts. The host is the habitat. Together host and parasite are one ecosystem. As one changes, so does the other.

What would happen if all *Anopheles* mosquitoes were destroyed? Would the malaria plasmodium be picked up and carried to hosts by some other insect? Or would malaria cease to exist? Hemetin from leeches helps doctors treat heart attack victims. Will we find other parasites that make some substance for their own survival that we might put to use for humans? Can we change viruses, bacteria, and other destructive parasites into beneficial organisms? Scientists have only just begun to unravel the complex interconnections that make one organism a host and another a parasite, and it is likely there will be amazing discoveries in this area for a long time to come.

# GLOSSARY

**altricial:** a species of animal, especially birds, in which the young are helpless and blind when hatched and need to be fed and cared for by an adult bird.

**amoeba:** a one–celled animal that moves by forming temporary projections called pseudopods that are constantly changing shape.

**arachnid:** an eight-legged animal such as a spider, tick, scorpion, or mite.

**cellulose:** a substance that forms the cell walls of plants; the woody part of trees and plants.

**cercaria:** the parasitic larva of a fluke.

**dormant:** inactive; in a state of rest.

**down:** the fine, soft, fluffy feathers of a young bird.

**ectoparasite:** a parasite that lives outside a host.

**endoparasite:** a parasite that lives within a host.

**entomology:** the scientific study of insects.

**flagellum:** a long, whiplike tail on some protozoans that allows them to move.

**host:** a living animal or plant in or on which a parasite lives.

**host specific:** a parasite adapted to live in or on a specific host plant or animal.

**hyperparasite:** a parasite that lives in or on another parasite.

**larva:** the wormlike, young form of an insect that looks very different from the adult; may be a grub, maggot, or caterpillar.

**mutualism:** a partnership in which two species of plants or animals live together in a way that helps both species and harms neither of them.

**night soil:** a fertilizer consisting of solid human waste, which is rich in nitrogen.

**parasite:** a plant or an animal that lives in or on another organism from which it gets its food and sometimes shelter.

**parasitism:** a partnership in which two species of plants or animals live together and one animal benefits while the other is harmed.

**parasitology:** the scientific study of parasites and parasitism.

**plasmodium:** the protozoan that causes malaria.

**precocial:** a species of animal, especially birds, in which the young are covered with down and able to care for, feed, and move around freely by themselves as soon as they hatch.

**protoplasm:** the mixture of proteins, fats, water, and other substances that forms the living matter of all living cells.

**protozoan:** a microscopic, one–celled animal, such as an amoeba or a plasmodium.

**pseudopod:** a temporary projection of protoplasm that makes it possible for some one-celled organisms to move.

**scabies:** a skin disease, characterized by an irritating rash and itching, caused by mites burrowing under the skin.

**schistosome:** a parasite that may live in the blood of humans and other mammals; also known as a blood fluke.

**symbiosis:** a partnership between different species such as parasitism and mutualism.

**virology:** the scientific study of viruses and viral diseases.

**zoology:** the scientific study of animals and animal life.

# FURTHER READING

Brimner, Larry D. *Unusual Friendships: Symbiosis in the Animal World.* New York: Watts, 1993.

Facklam, Margery. *Partners for Life: The Mysteries of Animal Symbiosis.* San Francisco: Sierra Club Books, 1989.

Gittleman, Ann Louise. *Guess What Came to Dinner: Parasites and Your Health.* Garden City Park, New York: Avery, 1993.

Halton, Cheryl M. *Those Amazing Leeches.* New York: Dillon Press, 1990.

Labonte, Gail. *Leeches, Lampreys, and Other Cold-blooded Bloodsuckers.* New York: Watts, 1991.

Silverstein, Alvin, et. al. *Lyme Disease, the Great Imitator: How to Prevent and Cure It.* Lebanon, New Jersey: Avstar, 1990.

# INDEX

Dutch elm disease, 48
dysentery, 44

ectoparasites, 21, 29, 58
eelworms, 10
endoparasites, 29, 32, 59
Entamoeba gingivalis, 7
Entamoeba histolytica, 44
entomology, 18, 59
epilepsy, 34
*Escherichia coli (E. coli)* bacteria, 7, 9, 49

flagella, 42, 44, 45, 59
flatworms, 12, 28, 36
flies, 12, 15, 43, 46
flukes, 10, 28, 29, 30, 31
fungi, 12, 48, 50

Giardia, 16, 42, 43, 44
grape mildew, 48
Gulf War, 14, 46

hematin, 23, 57
hirudin, 22, 23, 25
honeyguide birds, 55
hookworms, 12, 39
hosts, 7, 9, 10, 11, 12, 16, 21, 23, 25, 27, 28, 29, 31, 32, 34, 37, 38, 45, 46, 48, 51, 53, 54, 57, 59
hyperparasites, 7, 59

immune system, 50
imprinting, 55
insecticides, 46

*Journal of the American Medical Association*, 12

kala-azar or leishmaniasis, 46, 47

leeches, 21, 22, 23, 24, 25, 57
Leuckart, Karl Rudolph, 17, 18
Lyme disease, 25
lymph glands, 44

malaria, 45, 46, 57
measles, 48
mistletoe, 12
mosquitoes, 12
mutualism, 8, 9, 59

Navratilova, Martina, 16
nervous system, 27, 34, 44
*New Guinea Tapeworms and Jewish Grandmothers, Tales of Parasites and People,* 34, 35
night soil, 31, 32, 59

oysters, 11, 12

*Parasites of Man, The,* 17
parasitic insects, 10, 12
parasitic mites, 10, 12, 25, 26
parasitic worms, 10, 11, 12, 31
parasitology, 16, 17, 18, 60
pearls, 11, 12
pied wagtail, 55